The Prepper's Guide To Off The Grid Survival

An Introduction To Living A Stress Free, Self-Sustaining Lifestyle In Financial Peace

By Jim Jackson

Disclaimer

This book is intended to be a general guide, to raise awareness, and to help people make informed decisions in the context of their own personal circumstance.

The author accepts no responsibility for any loss or injury be it personal or financial, as a result for the use or misuse of the information in this book. If you have any doubts or concerns after reading this book, please speak to a qualified person before taking any actions.

Contents

Introduction

Chapter 1
The Benefits Of Off The Grid Living

Chapter 2
Alternatives To City Gas Water And Electricity

Chapter 3
Growing Your Own Fruits, Vegetables And Herbs

Chapter 4
Living With Small Livestock

Chapter 5
Money Management Tips And Bartering

Chapter 6
Dealing With Local Laws

Conclusion

Introduction

There is something to be said of being financially independent. How many nights do you lie awake at night worried about money? Worrying about how you will put food on the table for your family or how you will pay the electric bill. Constant worry and stress degrades your quality of life. Instead of doing the things you enjoy, you are too busy worrying about money matters.

It isn't just you that is affected by the worries of not having enough money. Your whole family feels the strain. What if you could learn to live with less? What if you could relieve your financial stress by learning to be self-sufficient? Wouldn't you jump at the chance?!

It is possible to learn a new way of life that gives you that financial freedom you are craving. You don't have to give up everything you love in life or do without. In fact, many people who have decided to go off the grid and become self-sufficient have found their lives are more fulfilling. There is plenty of food on the table and the comfort in knowing there is more where it came from and the fact that it is from your own backyard gives you peace of mind to know that it is safe.

When you live a self-sustaining lifestyle, you don't have to worry about where you will get the money to buy dinner for the kids or worry about food prices skyrocketing. You are removing that from the equation when you decide to grow and raise your own food.

Are you ready to learn about a lifestyle that will ultimately leave you happier and healthier? Going off the grid is the answer. Are you prepared for the challenge? This book will help guide you through some of the basics of what it takes to go off the grid.

Chapter 1
The Benefits Of Off The Grid Living

The benefits to living off the grid are probably far more than you would have expected. You are probably thinking off the grid means living in a rundown shack without running water or electricity. You would be wrong. There are plenty of people who have made the transition to living off the grid who live in nice houses and they enjoy running water and lights. It is all about looking for alternatives to government, city and public resources. Think back to our ancestors who lived 100 years ago. Most of them didn't pay electric bills or water bills or have anybody come by to pick up their trash. They took care of their needs on their own.

If you have a vacant piece of land and are considering building a dwelling, renovated motorhomes and trailers can make great cabins as in many counties they don't require building permits and depending on how you go about it are very affordable.

They didn't need a lot to live and what they did need they either grew or raised themselves. It was much more hands-on back then. We have gotten away from that in our technologically-advanced world. To be perfectly honest, we are a bit lazy nowadays. When we are hungry, we go to the grocery store or a drive-thru to grab something to eat. We don't have to worry about cooking. We have it pretty easy. We don't have to wait for the corn to grow or worry about watering our garden so we can have a salad for lunch. We want it and we want it now. That has become the normal mentality. We freak out when we have to wait more than a couple of minutes for a complete meal. We eat food that isn't nutritious and is lacking in any real flavour because we are always in a hurry to get back to work or to get back to our fast-paced life.

STOP! Unplug and see what food really tastes like when it is actually cooked and not nuked. Take the time to watch the world around you instead of getting caught up in your own high-speed bubble. You don't know what you are missing.

When you choose to change your lifestyle, you are gaining not only financial freedom, but valuable skills. If there is ever a major event that throws our society back a couple hundred years in time, those that have already been honing their skills by living off the grid are going to come through the catastrophe with flying colours. For those not familiar with pumping their own water from a well, don't know their way around a solar power system or even experienced growing their own garden, this experience will be a struggle.

There are more and more people recognizing the need to return to our roots. We have had a fairly easy time of it the past hundred years or so. Our world is falling apart at the seams. Preppers recognize this and are doing what they can to get ahead of the game by preparing to live off the grid. Choosing to live off the grid and not being forced to live without services gives you the chance to learn and prepare for what the world will look like after a major event. Whether that event is war, civil unrest or a pandemic, we don't know. The key is being prepared for anything.

The following are a few more of the benefits you will gain when you take the leap into off the grid living.

- Save money on electricity bills. One of the biggest misconceptions about off grid living is the idea that the homes are miles outside of civilization. Actually, many people who choose to go off the grid are actually connected to the main power grid, but just opt not to use the service.
- Power outages are no longer an issue. If the power grid goes down, it won't bother you a bit. You will already have your backup power source.
- Alternative power is better for the environment. You are doing a little something to help reduce emissions and the draw on natural resources.
- You will discover you spend more quality time with your family. As you work together doing what is necessary to survive, you will bond. Planting in the garden or fixing fence lines gives you time to talk with your family members. You get to unplug!
- You will come to appreciate the little things in life. A sunrise, a sunset and a healthy spring storm all take on different meanings. You will literally have the chance to slow down and smell the roses. You will be working outside a great deal, which will put you in touch with nature.
- You will learn to do more with less. Financial freedom means putting away the credit cards. That means when something needs repairing, you will get creative. You are going to have to rely on your own ingenuity to make use of the things you have on hand.

There are literally hundreds of benefits to unplugging from the world. It is easy to get caught up in the rat race and lose touch with who you are. Taking a few steps back and learning about your loved ones and the beautiful earth we live in is important. You will begin to feel different and appreciate everything you do have a little bit more. For those who are spiritual, it will make you feel more spiritually content and complete.

Chapter 2
Alternatives To City Gas, Water And Electricity

If you are serious about going off the grid, you need to look for options to your current services. Natural gas, water and electricity are the main things to consider. You will also need to consider garbage service. If you live in the suburbs, you may have to keep up with garbage services. It is a nominal bill. Sanitation is far too important to skimp on. Sewer is another service that the government will not allow you to forego. It is a health risk. You HAVE to have proper sanitation in place or risk being forced out of your home by government officials.

Gas-If you want to use gas appliances, propane is an option. Large propane tanks can be set up on your property that will keep your oven, water heater, furnace and even your refrigerator functioning. The tank is filled as often as you need it. You will learn to monitor your propane usage in order to make it stretch. This gives you the flexibility to have a single bill that you would need to pay every few months depending on how much you used your propane. When you are paying a large bill, you

tend to be a little more frugal. Fortunately, the amount of propane you actually use to cook with is minimal. The bulk of your propane usage would be your furnace. This is why it is a good idea to look into wood heating as your main heat source. As you probably know, propane is a commodity that fluctuates and it can be anywhere from $3 a gallon to as high as $5 gallon. Most companies will have a minimum order for delivery. You will need to wait until your tank is close to empty to have it filled. Assume you have a 500-gallon tank, and you can see why those fill-ups hit the bank account pretty hard. You must learn to conserve. Wasting propane is literally like burning money.

Water-If you live in the suburbs, going off the grid for your water supply could be a little problematic. You will likely not be allowed to drill your own well. If you live on your own land, drilling your own well is an option, but it can be very expensive. If

Wells can provide you with a reliable source of water but just make sure you check you local laws before you start digging

you plan on living in your home for years to come, the initial price of the well will be offset by the monthly savings you will have by not paying a water bill. You will want to invest in either a solar pump or a hand pump to retrieve water from your well. Standard electric pumps are electricity hogs. Depending on what you are using for electricity, you may not always have enough electricity to run the pump.

Another option includes
using rain barrels and
cisterns with rainwater
catchment systems. You
can do this whether you
have a well or not.
However, as ridiculous
as it may sound, there
are a few counties that

have made collecting rainwater illegal. Yes, the counties
claim the rainwater is theirs and by catching it, you are
stealing. Fortunately, this is only in a handful of areas. You
can use rain barrels, which hold about 50 gallons of water
or go big and invest in large cisterns that can hold hundreds
of gallons of water. This is an ideal option if you live in a
place that gets significant rainfall. Fill several cisterns. You
never know when it will rain and you absolutely must have
water.

Water from streams, ponds and lakes should be avoided.
There are laws about using this water as your main source
of water for your home and quite frankly, you don't want it.
It is likely contaminated with human and animal waste and
a long list of chemicals from fertilizer run off. In a survival
situation, you could make that water safe to drink, but you
don't want to rely on it as your main source of water.

Electricity-Electricity is optional. There are plenty of folks
who live off the grid and do without electricity. It is
possible. However, if you like lights, running hot water and
cold food, you will need an alternative energy source. You
can stop using electricity in your home whether you are
smack dab in the middle of the city or out on a farm. Solar
power systems are widely available and are becoming more
and more popular as people make the switch in an effort to
be more environmentally friendly while saving money on

rising electric costs.

Solar is probably the most common. The systems are fairly easy to install and are always coming down in price. If you are considering going off the grid, you need to determine how many panels you need to power your home. If you are going to supplement your electricity with propane, you can get

Solar panels and getting cheaper all the time and are still the most viable way to get off the electricity grid for most situations

away with fewer panels. You will also want to learn new ways of doing without electricity. There are some handy people that have learned how to construct their own solar power systems for very little money. You can find plenty of tutorials about this on the internet. Keep in mind, these systems are typically designed with the idea of powering a few lights or a single key appliance and would not actually power the entire home.

Wind power is another option, but you will need space to install a turbine. There are typically city ordinances about the height of a given structure. A typical wind turbine would need to be 80-feet high, which is about two telephone poles stacked on top of

Wind turbines can provide you with grid free electricity but city ordinances can make installing one impractical also, they can be quite noisy which may make them less then ideal in a suburban environment

one another. You also need steady wind. Experts recommend an average wind speed of 12mph to get the most out of your wind turbine. If you live in an area where the wind seems to blow pretty steady, this is an option for you. Wind turbine systems are similar to solar power systems. You will need to place your turbine on a hill to maximize the wind power. There is some noise involved, which is a turn off for some. If you can place the turbine far enough away from your home and your neighbours, it shouldn't be an issue.

Hydro power is a last resort. Creating a hydro power system is cheaper, but you will need some mechanical skills to do so. Depending on the water source for your hydropower system, there may be days when you receive very little

Hydro power can provide you with grid free electricity provided you live close to a river or stream and it flows freely year round

electricity. You need a moving stream or river to generate power. If you live on your own land and have a natural stream moving downhill, you could feasible create a hydropower system. You would need a stream that moved at a rate of at least 2 gallons of water per minute with a steep drop or fast-moving water supply that didn't have a drop, but moved about 500 gallons of water per minute.

Chapter 3
Growing Your Own Fruits, Vegetables And Herbs

Gardening is a skill you absolutely must hone when you choose to go off the grid. For some, it comes natural while others will struggle a bit at first. Don't worry. Most plants are pretty easy to grow and do most of the work for you. Things like strawberries,  chives and cucumbers are prolific and you will soon realize you have more food than you could have hoped for.

Spend some time researching the art of companion planting. This is an excellent way to maximize space in your garden while giving your plants the nutrients needed to thrive, naturally. Planting peas that produce a lot of nitrogen next to nitrogen-loving tomatoes is just one example. There are some plants that absolutely loathe each other, like garlic and peas. You will want to avoid planting those items next to each other. Learning these basics will help you grow a garden that produces a bountiful harvest that you will use to feed your family. Planting climbing peas between stalks of corn is one way to take advantage of the tall corn stalks to use as stakes while providing the corn nitrogen. Peas like some shade and will thrive within the shady corn patch.

You will want to learn preservation techniques like canning, freezing and dehydrating as well. Once your garden really starts to take off, you will not be able to eat all your fresh produce before it goes bad. You certainly don't want it to go to waste either. Preserving your harvest ensures you have a well-stocked pantry all year until the next harvest season. In the dead of winter when you can pull out a can of your delicious sweet corn for dinner, you will be glad you did.

Learning how to grow your own food is one way you become more self-sufficient. You won't have to run to the grocery store and spend your hard-earned money buying things you can grow in your own backyard. There is a real sense of satisfaction when you can go out and pick the ingredients for a fresh salad for the dinner table or make a vegetable lasagne with items straight from your garden. It is like having your own grocery store in your backyard!

Part of your gardening process will include learning how to use free, natural fertilizers and compost. As part of your off the grid lifestyle, you will want to minimize the garbage you produce. Learning how to compost is one way to do that. A large part of the kitchen waste you would normally throw into the trashcan can be tossed into your compost pile. The compost breaks down and is then used to feed the soil in the garden, which helps ensure you have a healthy, prolific garden.

Vegetables and herbs are pretty easy to grow and even novice gardeners can experience the joy of having a producing garden. Fruits are a little more difficult. Strawberries are the exception. Some gardeners compare strawberries to weeds because they can get out of control. But strawberries are tasty treats that can be preserved for years, so it isn't usually an issue. People love strawberries and would likely be willing to buy them from you. In fact, most berries are fairly easy to grow and can be grown in any climate.

It is fruits like apples, oranges and pears that prove to be problematic. Where you live is going to influence what fruits you can grow. Fruit trees are finicky and the fruit requires a fairly long, warm growing season. If you live in a cool climate, this can be a problem. Fruit trees are also very susceptible to pests and blight. You need to do your homework and learn how to care for fruit trees before you invest the money into buying any.

With that said, you can compensate for a short growing season by constructing a green house. There are plenty of dwarf fruit tree varieties that can be grown in large containers placed in front of a large window in your home or in your greenhouse. These trees won't be as prolific as the fruit trees you see growing in an orchard, but they will produce fruit with a little tender, loving care.

Your greenhouse can also provide you with fresh vegetables all year round. You will need to invest in a heater for the greenhouse, but it can be done. If you live in an area with a short growing season, a greenhouse is the key to starting plants early and getting them in the garden to maximize the season. You can build a greenhouse out of inexpensive PVC pipe and plastic sheeting. Old sliding glass doors are another economical way to build a greenhouse.

Another option to extend the growing season is cold-frame boxes. These can be made with heavy-ply plastic sheeting or an old glass window. The boxes are an excellent way to grow root crops like potatoes, carrots, radishes and so on. There may be snow on the ground, but the sun will heat the glass and keep the ground underneath warm enough for the vegetables to thrive.

You will want to purchase heirloom seeds to start your garden with. This ensures you can use the seeds from the fruit and vegetables you grow to replant a fresh garden the following year. Most seed packs that are sold in stores are hybrids. They are crossbred to produce some of those speciality vegetables you see. Heirloom varieties are basically the most natural, unaltered seed form. Hybrid seeds cannot be used to grow vegetables that produce plants with seeds that can be replanted. While a few of the seeds may sprout, the likelihood of the plant producing edible vegetables is slim. If the plant does produce, it will likely not produce vegetables exactly like the first harvest.

Vegetables that have been bred to ripen faster or grow bigger, like the Early Girl tomato seed, will not produce tomatoes that have seeds inside that can be planted for next year. Save yourself some money by spending a little more on the heirloom varieties. You will never have to buy seeds again as long as you learn how to properly harvest and store the seeds.

If you are completely new to gardening, check into your local 4H or college extension office. There are often free or very affordable gardening classes offered. This is an excellent way to learn everything you need to know about growing your own food. Gardening isn't something you can just jump into without doing a little homework. Do not make the mistake of assuming it can't be that hard and then end up very hungry because your garden didn't grow.

Chapter 4
Living With Small Livestock

Small livestock are a key part to any off the grid living situation. Livestock provide a number of different resources. Small livestock would include chickens, goats, pigs and rabbits. If you live in a residential area, you will need to make sure it is legal for you to raise these animals. If you are on your own land, your only concern will be creating pens for your livestock.

Caring for livestock can be a fulltime job. Between your livestock and your garden, you will be able to take care of all of your food needs. The trick is to finding the right balance. Having more animals that you can care for is counterproductive. You will end up with sick animals that can wipe out your entire herd. It can also become quite costly to care for a lot of animals if they are not pulling their weight so to speak.

Raising livestock will require you to take care of feeding, water, cleaning out pens, maintaining pens and keeping the animals warm in the winter. Disease is a common problem and you will have to monitor your livestock carefully. You will need to educate yourself about how to cure some common ailments among livestock as well as how to prevent injury and disease from wiping out your livestock.

Every human and animal on your little homestead needs to serve a purpose. Raising animals just for the fun of it isn't feasible if you don't have the extra income to support it. This isn't to say cats and dogs are not useful. They are! Cats help control the mice population that could cause problems for your animals and dogs help keep away predators like coyotes, wolves and even large cats i.e. cougars and mountain lions.

Some of the more common small livestock and their uses are as follows.

Chickens-Chickens are fairly easy to raise and will replenish if you have a rooster. You will need to do some research into what it takes to hatch chicks. There are some breeds that simply don't make very good breeders. Chickens can be used for meat as well  as eggs. Choose the right kind of chicken based on its purpose. Most chickens used for meat purposes are butchered early on, around 6 months of age. Layer hens will produce eggs for several years depending on the breed. Rhode Island Reds are an ideal choice for your flock and can be used for meat birds or layers. However, the Red hens don't always make the best mothers. You may need to invest in an incubator to ensure you always have a fresh supply of new chicks being introduced into your flock. This is another way you can earn money. There are plenty of folks who will be willing to pay for your baby chicks.

Pigs-Pigs are used solely for their meat. Pigs are butchered fairly young as well. If you time it right, you can avoid supporting pigs through the winter. You would need to get piglets early in the spring and raise them through fall before butchering. Typically, a pig is butchered when it weighs around 250 pounds. That doesn't mean all of that is turned to edible meat. The average yield for a 250-pound hanging weight pig is about 145 pounds of meat. Use this number to calculate how much meat you need to support your family. If you have more than a few pigs ready for butcher, you may want to consider selling some of the meat if your family cannot eat it within a couple of years.

If you want to breed your pigs, you will need to build a pen that will keep the pigs warm through the winter. On a side note, pigs are social creatures. You need at least two to keep your pigs happy. Ensuring the pigs have access to fresh water is another concern if temperatures are below freezing. Pigs can be fed kitchen scraps along with a standard feed, which is usually corn. You can cut out the cost of the feed by growing your own corn to feed the pigs. This will take up quite a bit of space and is really only feasible if you have at least a couple acres of land. Pigs can also be fed the fruit and veggies from your garden that you don't eat. The total cost of the meat per pound varies from under $1 a pound to $4 a pound depending on what you feed the pigs, how much you pay for a young pig and who does the butchering and processing. You can take care of the last job and save yourself a couple hundred dollars by cutting and wrapping the meat yourself.

Goats-Goats are
typically used for milk
only, but some people
raise goats for meat. You
will need at least two
goats. They are a social
animal and a single goat
would become depressed
and the milk production
would come to a halt.
Goat milk serves many

purposes. It can be used for drinking, as well as making
soap and hand creams, which are considered a luxury.
Cheese, butter and yogurt can also be made from goat milk.
Goats are much easier and less expensive to raise than
cows, which makes them a favourite among homesteaders.
They require very little care and are extremely hardy
creatures. Goats can be an issue if you don't have space to
let them graze. They eat everything! If you have a garden,
you do not want your goats anywhere near it. They are great
for clearing fields of woody plants, which could be used as a
garden the following year.

Rabbits-If you have a
couple of breeding
rabbits, you have a
hundred! They are
prolific breeders given
the chance! This is why
many preppers have
rabbits as a backup food
source. Although rabbits
are not as big as chickens

or pigs, the steady supply of rabbits is what makes them a good meat option. They require very little care and are very inexpensive to raise after the cost of pens is factored in. There isn't a lot of work to breeding and raising rabbits. They take care of it all for you! However, if you had to choose between rabbits and pigs or rabbits and chickens, the latter are better choices simply because the amount of edible meat is going to be more. Rabbit meat is incredibly lean and does not provide a great deal of fat, which you need for survival. It is fine as a supplementary meat source, but it should not be your only source of food.

Chapter 5
Money Management Tips And Bartering

If you are planning on going completely off the grid, raising your own food and doing with what you have, your monthly budget needs is going to drop exponentially. However, there will still be some things you need to buy. You will need to monitor your every expense, right down to the penny.

Living off the grid, gardening and raising livestock requires a great deal of time. You will likely only be able to work part-time or will have to find a way to make money from home. One of the most common ways for a homesteading family to earn income is to sell part of their crops. If you raise animals, you can make a decent income selling the meat, especially if it is organic. This would require you to have honed your gardening skill in order to produce a prolific garden that will feed your family as well as produce enough for you to sell some things.

One way you can use your excess crops and meat is as a bartering tool. If you need a tractor fixed, your mechanic may be willing to take 15 pounds of pork in exchange for performing the work. Eggs from your chickens, strawberries from your garden and even the poop from the chicken coop can all be traded or sold. Chicken poop is an excellent natural fertilizer and people will pay for it! With the popularity of natural and organic increasing, many people are turning to local farmers for their meat, fruits and vegetables. They are willing to pay premium prices for the items, which translates to a lucrative income for you. Before you consider selling your food, make sure you have plenty to feed your family first. Selling your food for cash and then turning around and buying food at the grocery store would be counterproductive.

There are some other things you can do to cut down on your monthly expenses.

- Make or buy a solar oven. If you are using propane for your oven, this is an excellent way to conserve on propane. During the winter, use your wood stove as a cook top. You can fry eggs, bacon, percolate coffee and heat water on your wood stove. You will want to invest in some cast iron cookware to use on the stove.

- Invest in a solar water heater. Again, if you use propane, you can cut down your usage by relying on the sun's energy to heat your water.

- Repurpose old wood, fencing and even nails to build pens for your livestock. You can save hundreds of dollars in building costs by using what you find in junkyards and old scrap piles.

- Check Craigslist or your local paper for free items that you can use to build pens, enhance your garden area or even around the house. Old tubs and troughs are often listed as free for the taking, which you can use for container gardening.

- If you have a tractor, consider switching it to a biofuel. This is something that takes some practice and a lot of research. John Deere has recently gotten on board with the biofuel movement and supports using a blend of biofuel in their tractor's engines. This can save you a great deal of money on food costs.

- Maximize your land. Do you really need a big, green lawn that will use water without giving you anything to eat? Scale down to having a small lawn and use the rest of your land for raising livestock and growing food you can eat.

- Park your car. Plan once a week or once a month trips into town to pick up supplies. Walk or ride a bike if you are close enough. With high gas prices, you can't afford to run back and forth to pick up this or that. You need to save every penny.

- Do what you can to stay healthy. You can't afford to get sick. Medical bills are only half the problem. If you get sick, you will struggle to take care of your farm and livestock, which will greatly impact your food supply. You can save on medical costs by learning more about natural healing methods. There are plenty of herbs and plants you can grow in your own garden that can be used to treat a variety of ailments.

- Take advantage of any government tax breaks and subsidies that are offered for those who use alternative power. Farms that grow certain crops can also be eligible for tax incentives. You will need to check for any other tax breaks out there for using your rural land for farming.

Pinching pennies is the key to your success living off the grid. When you first start out on your journey to living off the grid, you are going to make some mistakes. Some of the most mistakes may involve how you handle your finances. It takes some adjustment to get used to living within a fairly tight budget. You will learn to mend socks rather than tossing them out to buy new ones. It is a complete change in lifestyle. You will have to learn to monitor every kilowatt of electricity you use and how much food you cook at a single meal. You cannot afford to throw out perfectly good food because you don't like it or you don't want to eat it.

Chapter 6
Dealing With Local Laws

As hard to believe as it may sound, there are plenty of counties across the nation that has made living off the grid an illegal activity. There are plenty of people who have tried to disconnect from city services only to be slapped with fines and threatened to be removed from their homes if they did not use city services. Unfortunately, those are the laws and unless you want to risk losing everything and paying through the nose to try to be financially free, you need to follow the laws.

Your best option is to arm yourself with knowledge. Read through the laws and talk with your county officials before you decide to unplug. You can save yourself a lot of trouble by finding ways around the law without actually breaking it. They are out there! Typically, the biggest problem county officials have is sewage and water hook-ups. All homes in a residential area are supposed to be hooked up to the city sewer or have their own certified septic tank. All homes must have running water as well. This is meant to be a law that protects others from the potential danger of human waste floating about.

If you live on your large piece of land, you won't have to worry as much about complying with the laws. Laws are a little more lax when you are outside city limits, but they are still there and can still be enforced.

Most of the laws will stipulate a person or family cannot live in a dwelling for more than a month or two without a sewer management system and running water. If you only have a small amount of money, it would be wise for you to dedicate it to installing some kind of cistern for running water and a septic tank with a proper drain field. If you try to skirt the law and skip these two things, you not only face mountains in fines, you could also end up being charged with a huge clean-up bill.

Yet another consideration is your water source. Rivers, lakes and other bodies of water are technically owned by the government. You cannot use the water for your own personal needs. You cannot hook pipes up to the local lake and run them into your home. As was mentioned earlier, large rain barrels or water catchment systems may also be illegal. Do your research before you invest in the equipment to make one of these systems.

The size of your home may also be questioned. Tiny homes are all the rage right now as people learn to live with less. It is all with the same goal in mind—to become financially free. Unfortunately, the government is pretty deadest against people taking such extreme action. Your home will have to be at least 200 square-feet. Some areas may require bigger.
There are always going to be laws and taxes. Failure to abide by the laws or pay the taxes on your home will end up

leaving you completely down and out. When you are considering going off the grid, you will want to spend a lot of time looking around for the right area for you. Don't spend a penny of your money trying to set up a home off the grid in an area that it isn't allowed.

Invest the money you have into buying a piece of land and setting it up to comply with the law. You will feel better and won't have to worry about code enforcement knocking on your door and inspecting every inch of your property. Certain outbuilding for your livestock may also fall under the laws of your county. Always check to be sure. Typically, if the buildings are considered temporary, you won't have to worry about getting permits.

Don't risk everything by trying to dodge the law. All it takes is a single phone call or an eager code enforcement officer to disrupt your entire life. Get informed and arm yourself with your rights.

Conclusion

Living off the grid and becoming financially free is a goal many people have. However, it isn't for everybody. There are going to be some really hard days when you long for the easy way of life. Those are the days when you need to really think about how easy it was. Was it easy feeling stressed about how you would pay the electric bill? Was it easy when you ended up paying twice as much for that new television because you put it on a credit card with a crippling interest rate? You have to put it all in perspective.

Living without debt is an absolutely amazing feeling. It makes getting out of bed in the morning to go milk the goat or feed the chickens a lot easier. You are not weighed down by the looming debt that is ready to pull you down. Your life is completely in your hands when you choose to go off the grid. You are responsible for taking care of your food, water and other needs. When you succeed, it is such a feeling of accomplishment you will wonder why you didn't take the leap earlier.

Spending time working alongside your family is amazing as well. You learn so much more about a person when you are put into situations that require you to work together and actually communicate without a cell phone or text messaging. Teenagers may grumble a bit at first, but you can take comfort in knowing you are teaching them a very valuable life lesson about learning to live without debt. The skills they will learn are also going to help them later in life. Learning that the good things in life are not always sold at the mall, is a valuable lesson your entire family will be able to benefit from....

Good luck to you and your journey to live in financial peace and off the grid!

From The Author

Thank you for taking the time to read this book. As an author, I understand the importance of creating books which my readers will find both enjoyable and informative. If you have the time and feel generous, please don't hesitate to leave an honest review of this book..........Jim Jackson

Other Book By Jim Jackson

The Death Of Money

Surviving an economic collapse requires that you be prepared. This small guide will enable you to formulate a plan, allowing you to be proactive instead of reactive to a catastrophic financial crisis. In four chapters, you will gain invaluable knowledge and insight into what it takes to ensure you and your family have the tools necessary to survive the devastating impact of the loss of paper assets. Discover the skills you need to withstand the perils of a vulnerable financial system.

Prepper's Pantry

Are you prepared in the event of an emergency? Do you have ample food storage to keep your family fed during a disaster? If not, then this book will guide you through the process of preparing for anything. These first steps in preparing your pantry will give you peace of mind knowing that you did what was necessary to care for your family. In this easy-to-read guide you will find information and facts you may have never considered and will gather valuable resources to sustain your family. The Prepper's Pantry can be the starting point for making sure your family can survive.

The Prepper's Grid Down Survival Guide

A major collapse of the power grid is inevitable. There are numerous scenarios that could cause a failed power grid that could leave large sections of the country or world in the dark. If you don't what could cause a massive power grid failure, you need to read the book. It isn't just the lights that go out.

Don't be embarrassed if you don't have the first clue about what you would do if you were plunged into a blackout. Many people don't, which is why you need this book. It will guide you through everything you need to know to stay alive in the event of a major power grid failure. You will learn some valuable tips that will help you prepare for the imminent failure of the power grid. There is no time like the present to start preparing your home and your family to live and ultimately thrive a disastrous event like a failed power grid. Stocking up today, could save your life tomorrow.

Camping And Cooking For Beginners

Everyone has a camping disaster story and rarely do they have anything to do with wild animals. From forgetting the food to discovering the tent is too small—a myriad of things can go wrong, but with Camping And Cooking For Beginners, your problems are solved. Beginning with the basics, this handy helper starts with a checklist of what you need for your trip.

Choosing the right tent, the right sleeping bag and how to start fires without matches (and he's not talking about rubbing two sticks together!) are only a few chapters in the book. The best advice is the authors Top Ten Mistakes First Time Campers Make (and how to avoid them!)—it is invaluable.